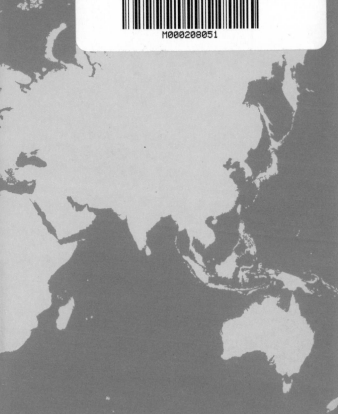

I Love You
You

POCKET TRANSLATOR

Published and distributed by Knock Knock
6080 Center Drive
Los Angeles, CA 90045
knockknockstuff.com
Knock Knock is a registered trademark of
Knock Knock LLC

This book is a work of humor meant solely for enter-
tainment purposes. In no event will Knock Knock
be liable to any reader for any damages, including
direct, indirect, incidental, special, consequential,
or punitive damages, arising out of or in connection
with the use of the information contained in this
book. So there.

ISBN: 978-168349124-8
UPC: 825703-50301-2

10 9 8 7 6 5 4 3 2

INTRODUCTION

Planet Earth is brimming with love, and this book is filled with ways to express it. Compiled with a far-flung team of linguistic consultants from Dubai to Shanghai, the *I Love You Pocket Translator* will enable you to speak the language of love wherever your globe-trotting heart may lead. All major world languages are included, as well as numerous smaller languages, some endangered. Planning to visit Paris, Jamaica, rural Paraguay, or remotest northern New Zealand? Pack your bags. (Just for fun, we've even included a few fictional languages.) Best of all, each phrase is presented with an easy-to-follow phonetic pronunciation, as well as a map to indicate the countries where it is most commonly spoken.

Be prepared: as you travel the world, it is entirely possible that you will discover romance, or at least a lusty facsimile of it. Travel is well known to improve people's moods, but it has also been proven to help improve people's sex lives. Of course, every region of the world has its own mores and attitudes toward romance, lust, flirtation, and Love-with-a-capital-L. "When we visit another country, we are their guests," says lawyer Frances Tibollo. "It's very prudent to inform yourself of the various laws and norms and practices."

Tibollo knows whereof she speaks: in 2018, she helped two young Canadian women gain release from a Cambodian prison after their arrest for "dancing pornographically." Tibollo chalked the incident up to "cultural misunderstanding," but added a word of caution against clueless tourism: "As a guest of a country, it's their rules."

With this sage advice in mind, you'll be free to venture forth with an open heart. Besides phrases, this book provides useful tips and fascinating insights about love around the world—like which countries get the most love, and how to express romantic interest without uttering a word.

You're a worldly person. You're a loving person. Now, with this small-but-mighty lexicon in your back pocket, you'll be an international lover—whether or not you ever leave home.

103 LANGUAGES

Afrikaans
Akan
Albanian
Amharic
Arabic
Armenian
Asturian
Azerbaijani
Basque
Belarusian
Bemba
Bengali
Bulgarian
Burmese
Cantonese
Catalan
Chewa
Czech
Danish

Dutch
Elvish
Esperanto
Estonian
Farsi
Finnish
Flemish
French
Galician
Georgian
German
Greek
Guarani
Haitian
Hausa
Hebrew
High
  Valyrian
Hindi

Hmong
Hungarian
Icelandic
Igbo
Indonesian
Irish
Italian
Jamaican
Japanese
Javanese
Kannada
Kazakh
Khmer
Kinyarwanda
Kirundi
Klingon
Korean
Ladino
Lao

Latvian	Russian	Welsh
Lithuanian	Serbian	Xhosa
Lombard	Sinhala	Yiddish
Macedonian	Slovak	Yoruba
Malagasy	Slovenian	Zulu
Malay	Somali	
Maltese	Spanish	
Mandarin	Sundanese	
Maori	Swahili	
Marshallese	Swedish	
Moldovan	Tagalog	
Mongolian	Tajik	
Nepali	Tamil	
Norwegian	Thai	
Oromo	Tigrinya	
Pashto	Tonga	
Pig Latin	Turkish	
Polish	Ukrainian	
Portuguese	Urdu	
Punjabi	Uzbekh	
Romanian	Vietnamese	

Ek het jou lief

(ak heht jo lihf)

Medɔ wo

(mee-dor woo)

Note: Akan is a tonal language and does not stress syllables.

COUNTRIES SPOKEN IN:

Côte d'Ivoire (Ivory Coast), Ghana

Unë të dua

(**oo**-neh tay doo-**ahh**)

COUNTRIES SPOKEN IN:

Albania, Italy, Kosovo, Macedonia, Montenegro, Serbia

Female recipient:

እወድሻለሁ
(ee-weh-dee-**shah**-leh-hoo)

Male recipient:

እወድሃለሁ
(ee-weh-dee-**ha**-leh-hoo)

COUNTRIES SPOKEN IN:
Ethiopia

Male recipient:

أُحِبُّكَ

(O-**heb**-boook-ahh)

Female recipient:

أُحِبُّكِ

(O-**heb**-boook-ee)

COUNTRIES SPOKEN IN:

Algeria, Bahrain, Chad, Comoros, Djibouti, Egypt, Iraq, Israel, Jordan, Kuwait, Lebanon, Libya, Mali, Mauritania, Morocco, Niger, Oman, Palestine, Qatar, Saudi Arabia, Somalia, Sudan, Syria, Tanzania, Tunisia, Turkey, United Arab Emirates, Yemen

Ես սիրում եմ քեզ

(yes **see-room** yem kezz)

COUNTRIES SPOKEN IN:

Armenia, Georgia, Iran, Lebanon, Russia,
Turkey, Ukraine

Quiérote

(kee-eh-oh-teh)

Səni sevirəm

(sah-nee seh-vee-ram)

Republic of Azerbaijan, Georgia, Iran, Iraq,
Russia, Turkey

LOVE, AMERICAN (AND CHINESE) STYLE

Perhaps it's no surprise that Americans say "I love you" more than people in many other countries, including China, where indirect expressions of affection are considered more sophisticated than blunt statements, an ethos rooted in the belief that actions speak louder than words. But things are changing, says UC Berkeley psychology professor Kaiping Peng, who came of age during Mao's Cultural Revolution. "*Wo ai ni*, or the Chinese equivalent of 'I love you,' is a thing of the last thirty years," he says. "Before then, you just showed love through holding hands, kissing, or maybe writing or doing something nice—but you never said it." Research shows that when young people come to study in the U.S. from abroad, they start saying "I love you" more—but they tend to say it in English more than in their native tongues. Somehow, "I love you" just rolls off the tongue—perhaps because, for many, it *lacks* cultural baggage.

♥

Maite zaitut

(**mah**-ee-tay-sah-ee-**toot**)

COUNTRIES SPOKEN IN:

Spain, France

Я цябе кахаю
(ya tsyah-beh ka-**kha**-yu)

Nalikutemwa

(nah-**lee**-koo-teh-mwah)

COUNTRIES SPOKEN IN:

Zambia, Democratic Republic of the Congo, Tanzania

আমি তোমাকে ভালবাসি

(**aah-mee** toh-mah-kay
bah-lo-bah-shee)

Обичам те
(oh-**bee**-cham teh)

ငါမင်းကိုချစ်တယ်

(naar min koh chit tal)

Note: Tones in Burmese are flat, therefore no
syllables are stressed.

我愛你

(no **oyy** nee)

COUNTRIES SPOKEN IN:

China

T'estimo

(tehz-**tee**-moo)

WHICH COUNTRIES GET THE MOST LOVE?

They say love makes the world go round. While this can't be scientifically proven, researchers have tried to quantify how much love goes round planet Earth every day. In 2006 and 2007, Gallup pollsters visited 136 countries and asked people if they had felt loved the previous day. The result, as economist Justin Wolfers describes it, was "the most comprehensive global index of love ever constructed." In the poll, about 70% of people said they had experienced love whether romantic, platonic, or familial. But not all countries appear to love equally. Armenia ranked last, while the Philippines ranked first. The U.S. ranked a respectable twenty-sixth. Wolfers warns that these differences may reflect how cultures define love: "For example, in some countries, the idea of 'love' is restricted to a romantic partner, while in others it extends to one's family members and friends." Or maybe the Philippines knows something we don't.

Ndimakukondani

(ndee-ma-koo-**koh**-nda-nee)

COUNTRIES SPOKEN IN:

Malawi, Mozambique, Zambia, Zimbabwe

Miluji tě
(mee-loo-**yee** tyeh)

COUNTRIES SPOKEN IN:

Czech Republic

Jeg elsker dig

(yai **el**-sker dah)

DUTCH

Ik hou van jou

(Eek **how** vun yow)

COUNTRIES SPOKEN IN:

The Netherlands, Belgium, Suriname, Aruba,
Curaçao, France, Sint Maarten

Le melin

(leh **meh**-leen)

COUNTRIES SPOKEN IN:

Rivendell and Lothlorien in J. R. R. Tolkien's
Middle-earth.

Mi amas vin

(mee **ah**-mas veen)

COUNTRIES SPOKEN IN:

China, Korea, Japan, Iran, Brazil, Argentina, Mexico, Togo

Ma armastan sind

(ma **ar**-ma-stan sind)

دوستت دارم
(doo-set dah-ram)

COUNTRIES SPOKEN IN:

Iran, Afghanistan, Tajikistan, Uzbekistan

Minä rakastan sinua

(**mee**-nah **ra**-kaah-stan **see**-nuh-a)

Ik zie u graag

(ick **see** oo-ghragh)

EVEN SEXIER THAN LOVE AT FIRST SIGHT?

In English, the notion of "love at first sight" is celebrated in story and song as a romantic ideal—much like the idea of being shot by Cupid's arrow. Yet for many of us, falling in love happens more gradually, with shades of nuance. The Japanese have a phrase that captures some of that subtlety: *Koi no yokan*, which may be translated as "a premonition of love." Rather than the full-bore impact of love at first sight, *koi no yokan* is "the feeling upon first meeting someone that you will inevitably fall in love with them," says Japanese language director Tomoyo Kamimura. One might think of it this way: love at first sight is like waking up in a hurricane. *Koi no yokan* is like walking out into the calm before the storm. It's no less momentous than love at first sight, and with the delicious suspense of delayed gratification—always a boon to romance.

♥

Je t'aime

(zhuh **tem**)

France, Belgium, Benin, Burkina Faso, Burundi, Cameroon, Canada, Central African Republic, Chad, Comoros, Côte d'Ivoire (Ivory Coast), Djibouti, Dominica, Equatorial Guinea, Gabon, Guinea, Haiti, Luxembourg, Madagascar, Mali, Monaco, Niger, Democratic Republic of the Congo, Republic of Congo, Rwanda, Santa Lucia, Senegal, Seychelles, Switzerland, Togo, Vanuatu

Quérote

(**ke**-roh-teh)

COUNTRIES SPOKEN IN:

Spain

მე შენ მიყვარხარ

(meh shen **mik-var-khar**)

COUNTRIES SPOKEN IN:

Georgia

Ich liebe Dich

(eesh **lee**-buh deesh)

Austria, Belgium, Germany, Liechtenstein,
Luxembourg, Switzerland

Σε αγαπώ

(se aga-**po**)

COUNTRIES SPOKEN IN:

Cyprus, Greece

Rohayhu

(ro-high-**hoo**)

Paraguay, Argentina, Brazil, Bolivia

Mwen renmen w
(mweh **reh**-meh'w)

COUNTRIES SPOKEN IN:
Haiti

Ina son ki

(ee-na **son** kee)

Niger, Nigeria, Ghana, Benin, Cameroon, Côte
d'Ivoire (Ivory Coast), Sudan

I JUST ~~CALLED~~ TEXTED TO SAY "143"

Some romantic text-messaging symbols far predate digital technology (e.g., XOXO, SWAK). But many codes for "I love you" have been devised based on the telephone keypad—including these:

459: Each number indicates the telephone key for "I Love You."

831: Stands for "8 letters, 3 words, 1 meaning."

143: Each number indicates the number of letters in each word of "I love you."

1432: Means "I love you, too."

286: This number represents 143 (or "I Love You") times 2.

Acronyms and emoticons are even more popular than numbers. The options below represent just a fraction of romantic texting phrases in current usage.

BB: Baby   **ILY:** I love you   **4EVA:** Forever

<3: Emoticon representing a heart

BAE: Babe, baby

HEBREW

Female to male:

אני אוהבת אותך

(ah-**nee** oh-**hev**-et oht-**kha**)

Male to female:

אני אוהב אותך

(ah-**nee** oh-**hev** oht-**takh**)

Female to female:

אני אוהבת אותך

(ah-**nee** oh-**hev**-et oht-**takh**)

Male to male:

אני אוהב אותך

(ah-**nee** oh-**hev** oht-**kha**)

Avy jorrāelan

(ah-vee jo-rye-luh)

COUNTRIES SPOKEN IN:

In *Game of Thrones*, the continent of Essos, Valyria (now gone)

Male speaker:

मैं तुमसे प्यार करता हूँ

(mae toomsay pyaar karta hoon)

Female speaker:

मैं तुमसे प्यार करती हूँ।

(mae toomsay pyaar kar-tee hoon)

COUNTRIES SPOKEN IN:

India

Kuv hlub koj

(koo loo **kaw**)

COUNTRIES SPOKEN IN:

China, Vietnam, Laos, Myanmar, Thailand

Szeretlek

(ser-et-lek)

Ég elska þig

(yey **els**-kah thih)

COUNTRIES SPOKEN IN:
Iceland

A hụrụ m gị n'anya

(ah-**huroom** ginah-nya)

Aku cinta kamu

(ah-koo **cheen**-ta **kaa**-mu)

COUNTRIES SPOKEN IN:

Indonesia

Tá mé i ngrá leat

(tah-maing rah-let)

Ti amo

(tee **ah**-mo)

WHAT THE WORLD NEEDS NOW = MORE SEX

If you ever feel that your love life has gotten a bit meh, rest assured: you're not alone. *Time* reported in 2016, "Sexual frequency has declined globally in the past few decades, even before Netflix." Only 44% of people around the world are fully satisfied in bed, according to the Durex Global Sexual Wellbeing Survey (which quizzed 26,000 people in 26 countries). Not surprisingly, stress—often known as "the modern disease"—has a profound effect on sexual frequency and satisfaction. This may explain why Japan, famous for its stressed-out workforce, ranked at the bottom of the survey. The countries who reported the greatest sexual satisfaction were Brazil, Greece, Italy, the Netherlands, Nigeria, Spain, and Switzerland. But if you don't live in one of those lucky places, here's a bit of advice. According to a 2016 Cornell University study, the couples who have the most sex all have one thing in common: they share housework and childcare duties. Gentlemen, start your vacuums.

♥

Mi love yuh

(mee **luv** yuh)

COUNTRIES SPOKEN IN:

Jamaica

大好き

(die-skee)

Aku tresna sampeyan

(aku **tres-nah sam**-pee-en)

COUNTRIES SPOKEN IN:

Indonesia, Suriname

ನಾನು ನಿನ್ನನ್ನು
ಪ್ರೀತಿಸುತ್ತೀನ್

(**nah**-noo nih-nah-noo
prih-tee-suh-**tee**-nay)

Мен сені сүйемін

(men **seh**-nee soo-**ee**-min)

COUNTRIES SPOKEN IN:

Kazakhstan

ខ្ញុំស្រលាញ់អ្នក

(khnum sro-lan nyeh)

Note: Tones in Khmer are flat, therefore no syllables are stressed.

Cambodia

Ndagukunda

(ndah-**goo**-koon-dah)

COUNTRIES SPOKEN IN:

Rwanda

Ndagukunda

(ndah-goo-koo-ndah)

COOK UP A LITTLE CHEMISTRY—NO WORDS REQUIRED!

When facing a romantic language barrier, you can always try nonverbal methods to kindle excitement. Besides the obvious—sharing food and drink—you might try a museum date. The Roman Institute of Psychology found that 1 in 5 visitors to Italy's museums was inspired to have an "erotic adventure" inside. This phenomenon is known as Rubens Syndrome, named for the famed painter of curvaceous nudes, and has been characterized as a type of "emotional arousal" or "cultural seduction." Another idea: take your special friend on a roller coaster, speedboat ride, or other heart-pounding adventure. According to the Schachter-Singer theory, when people are placed in situations that feel dangerous, they can mistake their racing heartbeat and rapid breathing for physical chemistry with their companion. Guess they're called hot rods for a reason.

♥

bangwI' SoH

(bahng-wee shokh)

COUNTRIES SPOKEN IN:

Star Trek's Klingon Empire

사랑해

(sah-rang-hae)

COUNTRIES SPOKEN IN:

South Korea, North Korea

טי אמו
(teh-**ah**-moh)

ຂ້ອຍຮັກເຈົ້າ

(khoi hook **jao)**

Es tevi mīlu

(es teh-vee mee-loo)

Aš tave myliu

(**ahsh** tah-veh **mee**-loo)

Lithuania

Ti amo

(tee **ah**-moh)

Italy, Switzerland

Те сакам

(tay **saah**-kahm)

Tiako ianao

(tee-koo ye-now)

Aku
cinta kamu

(uh-**coo** chin-**tuh kuh**-moo)

SAY IT WITH FLOWERS

For eons people have used flowers to convey love—useful when open expression might have been improper or impossible. In Japan the art of *hanakotoba* assigns meanings to blooms: camellias mean you're in love; cactus flowers signal lust. During the Ottoman Empire, it is believed a coded language developed in Turkish harems. The practice, sometimes called *selam*, conveyed messages with fruit and flowers—and helped to inspire the European tradition of using flowers to send romantic messages. This practice peaked in the Victorian era with publication of the classic *The Language of Flowers*, but lives on. Princess Kate Middleton's bridal bouquet included ivy (symbolizing marriage), sweet William (denoting gallantry, and a nod to her beloved's name), and lily of the valley (which *The Language of Flowers* says means a return to happiness).

Inħobbok

(**in**-hob-bok)

COUNTRIES SPOKEN IN:

Malta

我爱你

(wo ai nee)

E aroha ana ahau ki a koe

(eh aroha anah **ahau** kee ah k**o-eh**)

New Zealand, Cook Islands

Ij iakwe eok

(eej **yok**-weh-yoke)

Marshall Islands

Te iubesc

(tay **yoo**-besk)

COUNTRIES SPOKEN IN:

Moldova

Би чамд хайртай

(beẹ tchamd kai-eer-tai)

Mongolia

म तिमीलाई माया गर्छु

(mah timmy-lai
maya gar-chhoo)

COUNTRIES SPOKEN IN:

Nepal

Jeg elsker deg

(yai **els**ker dai)

SPEAK FLUENT SEXY TALK

Travel broadens your horizons—in more ways than one. The Kinsey Institute found that time off enables the part of the brain that suppresses sexual response to recede and the activating part to step forward. While traveling, you'll want to have a few flirty phrases handy.

Believe it or not, these are genuinely romantic terms of endearment:

- **Chinese:** *Chen yu luo yan* ("Diving fish/ swooping geese")
- **French:** *Ma puce* ("My flea")
- **Japanese:** *Tamago gata no kao* ("Egg with eyes")

If you're feeling audacious, consider one of these cheeky phrases:

- **Italian:** *Tu è così grande* ("You are so big")
- **French:** *Je suis si chaude* ("I am so horny")
- **Spanish:** *Quítese la ropa* ("Take your clothes off")

♥

Siin jaaladha

(seen jala-dha)

زه درسره مينه لرم
(za tah-sarah meena laram)

COUNTRIES SPOKEN IN:

Afghanistan, Pakistan

Iyay ovelay ouyay

(ai-yay uvv-lay ooh-yay)

COUNTRIES SPOKEN IN:

United States, Canada, United Kingdom,
Australia, New Zealand

Kocham cię

(**ko**-ham che)

COUNTRIES SPOKEN IN:

Poland

Eu te amo

(eh-oo **chee** uh-moo)

Male speaker:

ਮੈਂ ਤੁਹਾਨੂੰ ਪਿਆਰ ਕਰਦਾ ਹਾਂ

(main-tuha-nu-pee-aar
kah-rah-dah-haan)

Female speaker:

ਮੈਂ ਤੁਹਾਨੂੰ ਪਿਆਰ ਕਰਦੀ ਹਾਂ

(main-tuha-nu-pee-aar
kah-rah-dee-haan)

COUNTRIES SPOKEN IN:

India, Pakistan

Te iubesc

(tey **yoo**-besk)

Я тебя люблю
(ya teb-**ya** lyoo-blee**yoo**)

COUNTRIES SPOKEN IN:

Russia, Belarus, Kazakhstan, Ukraine

Volim te

(voh-leem teh)

Serbia, Bosnia and Herzegovina, Kosovo, Montenegro

මං ඔයාට
ආදරෙයි

(maamuh **oyah-**
tuh ah da-reh)

Sri Lanka

BODY LANGUAGE AROUND THE WORLD

Words aren't the only way to communicate your feelings: body language signals (at least) half your message. Anthropologist Helen E. Fisher says that women signal interest with a notably similar sequence of expressions: First, smile and lift your eyebrows in a swift motion, and open your eyes to gaze at your admirer. Then drop your eyelids, tilt your head down and to the side, and look away. A few other body-language tips to keep in mind while traveling:

- **Asia:** Avoiding eye contact is a sign of respect. Densely populated nations generally have less need for personal space.

- **Latin America:** Eye contact is utilized to establish equality among individuals. Winking is considered flirtatious or romantic.

- **Middle East:** Showing the bottom of the shoe is considered disrespectful, including sitting with the foot resting on the opposite knee. Using the left hand to accept a gift or shake hands is considered rude.

♥

Milujem ťa

(mee-loo-**yem** tya)

COUNTRIES SPOKEN IN:

Slovakia

Ljubim te

(lyu-beem teh)

COUNTRIES SPOKEN IN:
Slovenia

Waan ku jeclahay

(ˈwan-koo-jeˈ-la-hi)

Note: Apostrophes represent a scratchy "krr" throat sound vibrating at the top and back of the mouth.

COUNTRIES SPOKEN IN:

Somalia, Djibouti, Ethiopia

Te amo

(teh **ah**-moh)

COUNTRIES SPOKEN IN:

Argentina, Bolivia, Colombia, Chile, Costa Rica,
Cuba, Dominican Republic, Ecuador, El Salvador,
Equatorial Guinea, Guatemala, Honduras,
Mexico, Nicaragua, Panama, Paraguay, Peru,
Puerto Rico, Uruguay, Venezuela, Spain

Abdi bogoh ka anjeun

(**ahb-dee** bogo-kah ahn-jen)

COUNTRIES SPOKEN IN:

Indonesia

Ninakupenda
(nee-nah-**koo**-pen-**dah**)

Burundi, Democratic Republic of Congo, Kenya,
Rwanda, Tanzania, Uganda

"LOVE" IN JAPANESE? IT'S COMPLICATED

It's not easy to say "I love you" in Japan, for several reasons. Japanese culture avoids overt declarations of love, and openly saying "I love you" can be a source of embarrassment. Perhaps because of this, Japanese has many idioms that more or less mean "I love you," but which contain and specify the emotions being expressed. You could call it an "I love you" spectrum, with phrases ranging from lighthearted (*suki da yo*) to I-want-to-die-together (*ai shiteru*). To make things more complex, Japanese also has different words for love in its early, lusty stage (*koi*) and its later, deeper stage (*ai*). Choosing the right phrase is a challenge with high stakes. If you'd like to play it safe, show your feelings through a gift or other non-verbal expression—these are as highly prized as any words, and perhaps more so.

♥

Jag älskar dig
(yaah **els**-koor dey)

Sweden, Finland

Mahal kita

(ma-haal **kee**-ta)

Philippines

Ман туро дӯст медорам

(man **too-roh** doost medoram)

நான் உன்னைக் காதலிக்கிறேன்

(naan **ooh**-nyke **kaad**-**ha**-leek-keer-ain)

COUNTRIES SPOKEN IN:

India, Sri Lanka

Male speaker:

ผมรักคุณ
(pom **raak** koon)

Female speaker:

ฉันรักคุณ
(chan **raak** koon)

COUNTRIES SPOKEN IN:

Thailand

Male recipient:

የፍቅረካ'የ

(yeff-kuh-ruh-kai-yeh)

Female recipient:

የፍቅረኪ'የ

(yeff-kuh-ruh-kee-yeh)

COUNTRIES SPOKEN IN:

Eritrea, Ethiopia

'Ofa Atu

(oh-fah ah-too)

Seni seviyorum

(**seh**-nee
sev-ee-**yoh**-room)

COUNTRIES SPOKEN IN:
Turkey, Cyprus, Northern Cyprus

Я кохаю тебе

(ya **koh**-kha-yoo **teh**-beh)

مجھے تم سے محبت ہے

(moo-jay tum say
moo-haab-bat hey)

COUNTRIES SPOKEN IN:

Pakistan, India

WORDS OF LOVE

French is rightfully known as the language of love. Still, many languages have deeply resonant terms for love—words that even seem to express emotions through their sound, a kind of onomatopoeia of the heart.

- **Viraag** (Hindi): The pain of separation or alienation from a loved one.

- **Onsra** (Boro language of India): knowing a love will end; loving for the last time.

- **Saudade** (Portuguese): Intense, haunted longing for a person or place.

- **Achai** (Tamil): Ardent longing.

- **Kara sevda** (Turkish): Literally translated as blind or black love, it describes passionate and destructive love.

- **Cavoli riscaldati** (Italian): Literally translated as "reheated cabbage," this refers to an attempt to revive an old romance.

- **Anurakti** (Sanskrit): Adoration, love, devotion.

- **'Ishq** (Arabic): Deriving from the Arabic word for "vine," it means deep love.

♥

Men seni sevaman

(men **seh**-nee **seh**-vah-munn)

COUNTRIES SPOKEN IN:

Uzbekistan

Male recipient:

Mình yêu anh

(ming eww **un**)

Female recipient:

Mình yêu em

(ming eww **am**)

COUNTRIES SPOKEN IN:

Vietnam

Dw i'n dy garu di

(dwin-dih duh **gaar**-ih dee)

COUNTRIES SPOKEN IN:

Wales

Ndiyakuthanda

(ndee-ya-koo-**taan-dah**)

איך האָב דיך ליב

(ikh hob dikh **lib**)

Mo nífẹ̀ rẹ

(mo ni feh reh)

Nigeria, Benin, Togo

Ngiyakuthanda

(**nghee**-yah-**koo**-**taan**-dah)

COUNTRIES SPOKEN IN:

South Africa

I Love You

POCKET TRANSLATOR

An Affectionate Lexicon

**Southern/
Mediterranean
Europe**
Catalan
French
Galician
Greek
Italian
Ladino
Lombard
Maltese
Spanish

**Southeastern
Europe**
Albanian
Bulgarian
Greek
Macedonian
Romanian
Serbian
Slovenian

**Western
Africa**
Akan
French
Hausa

Igbo
Yoruba

**Northern
Africa**
Arabic
French

**Central
Africa**
Bemba
French
Hausa
Kinyarwanda
Kirundi
Swahili

**Eastern
Africa**
Amharic
Arabic
Bemba
French
Kinyarwanda
Kirundi
Oromo
Somali
Swahili

Tigrinya

**Southeastern
Africa**
Chewa
Malagasy
Swahili

**Southern
Africa**
Afrikaans
Swahili
Xhosa
Zulu

**Middle East &
Western Asia**
Arabic
Armenian
Azerbaijani
Farsi
Georgian
Hebrew
Ladino
Oromo
Turkish
Yiddish
(continued)

LANGUAGES BY REGION

Central Asia
Azerbaijani
Farsi
Kazakh
Pashto
Russian
Tajik
Uzbek

Eastern Asia
Cantonese
Hmong
Japanese
Korean
Mandarin
Mongolian
Uzbek

Southern Asia
Bengali
Hindi
Kannada
Nepali
Pashto
Punjabi
Sinhala
Tamil
Urdu

Southeastern Asia
Burmese
Cantonese
Hmong
Indonesian
Javanese
Khmer
Lao
Malay
Sundanese
Tagalog
Thai
Vietnamese

Australia/New Zealand
Maori
Tonga

Micronesia & Polynesia
Marshallese
Tonga

LANGUAGES BY REGION

A geographic breakdown of where this book's languages are primarily spoken.

North America
French
Yiddish

Central America
Spanish

South America
Brazilian
Guarani
Portuguese
Spanish

Caribbean
Dutch
French
Haitian
Jamaican Patois
Spanish

Western Europe
Asturian
Basque
Dutch
Flemish
French
Galician
German
Irish
Italian
Lombard
Spanish
Welsh

Northern Europe
Danish
Estonian
Finnish
Icelandic
Latvian
Lithuanian
Norwegian
Swedish

Central Europe
Czech
German
Hungarian
Slovak

Eastern Europe
Azerbaijani
Belarusian
Georgian
Kazakh
Moldovan
Polish
Russian
Serbian
Ukrainian
Yiddish